# CLEOPATRA
## QUEEN OF KINGS

Written by
### A.R. AZZAM
&
### Illustrated by
### LAURA DE LA MARE

HOOD HOOD BOOKS

Copyright © Hood Hood Books 1998

Hood Hood Books
46 Clabon Mews
London SW1X OEH

Tel: 44 171 584 7878
Fax: 44 171 225 0386

British Library Cataloguing–in–Publication Data
A catalogue record for this book is available from the British Library

ISBN 1 900251 28 0

Origination by: Fine Line Graphics-London.
Printed by IPH-Egypt.

# CLEOPATRA

Cleopatra was Egypt's last and most famous queen. Her real title was Cleopatra VII, but such was her fame that the previous six Cleopatras have been wiped off the pages of history – leaving only one Cleopatra.

In an age of war and bloodshed, Cleopatra used her powerful intelligence, her beauty and charm to defend her country. Also, the two most powerful men of the day, Julius Caesar and Mark Antony, fell in love with her. For the tale of Cleopatra is the tale of a mighty empire, an ancient land, two Roman generals and the beautiful Queen of Egypt.

Although people think of Cleopatra as being Egyptian, Egypt being the place where she was born, lived and died, she was in fact of Greek origin. She came from a Greek dynasty, or ruling family, called the Ptolemies, the first of whom was one of Alexander the Great's generals. It was Alexander the Great who founded the city of Alexandria on the Mediterranean coast of Egypt in around 300 B.C. Cleopatra, born a princess in 70 B.C., was brought up in the Royal Palace at Alexandria, which by that time had become the capital of Egypt.

Egypt was the jewel of the ancient world. On the banks of the Nile beautiful reeds grew from which a kind of paper called papyrus was made. Also, the fertile Nile Valley made Egypt the world's biggest producer of grain. But Egypt's power had waned and had become overshadowed by the new power in the region – Imperial Rome. From her earliest years Cleopatra was always aware of the threat that one day one of the rulers in Rome would seek to take over her country and add it to their empire.

Even as a child it was clear that Cleopatra was a person of exceptional intelligence who learned very fast. When she was young her father taught her several African and Eastern languages, including Hebrew and Aramaic. In fact, Cleopatra was the only member of the ruling Ptolemies who ever learned the language of the Egyptian people they ruled.

In 60 B.C. when Cleopatra was ten years old, her father, Ptolemy XII, paid a state visit to Rome which was under the rule of the great Julius Caesar. While he was away, however, Berenice, Cleopatra's older sister, rebelled against her father and seized the throne of Egypt, leaving her father stranded in Rome.

It was not until the year 55 B.C. that Ptolemy persuaded Rome to send an army to help him regain his throne from his daughter. Roman forces now advanced into Egypt and were met by a large army under the command of Berenice and her husband, Archelaus. The battle was fierce and it was only after a brilliant cavalry charge by a young officer that it was won for the Romans. So, after five years of rule, Berenice and Archelaus were executed, Ptolemy was restored to his throne and Cleopatra was made his heir. But that is not the end of this story, for the name of the young officer was Mark Antony. So Cleopatra met the love of her life for the first time when she was only fifteen years old and he was nearly thirty.

Two years later Ptolemy died and Cleopatra became Queen of Egypt. Like the two queens many centuries before her, Hatshepsut and Nefertiti, her title became "Lady of the Two Lands", referring to Upper and Lower Egypt. On succeeding to the throne, however, Cleopatra was faced with a bleak future. The country was bankrupt and heavily in debt to Rome.

Everywhere there were plots and intrigues. Cleopatra was quick to discover that power turns friends into enemies and allies into rivals. After a particularly bad harvest in the year 50 B.C., a rebellion against her was organized by a certain Pothinus, and the Queen had to flee Egypt and seek refuge in the nearby port of Ascalon in Palestine.

Cleopatra watched helplessly as Pothinus seized her throne. In desperation she sent an urgent message to Caesar appealing for aid, and shortly afterwards news of his landing on Egyptian soil reached her. She was overjoyed that the great Julius Caesar had responded to her message so quickly. But she was not a fool and was well aware that her life was in extreme danger; hired assassins were plentiful and Pothinus had placed a high price on her head. Return to Egypt she must; the question was how?

Her arms behind her back, her head bowed deep in thought, Cleopatra paced up and down the room which served as her makeshift Royal Chamber in Ascalon. Suddenly, she stopped, seized by a thought. She clapped twice and her attendant came rushing in.

"We will sail for Egypt at once," she commanded, "for we must arrive in Alexandria under cover of night. We will travel light – myself and three attendants and we will take nothing more than our personal possessions and this." Cleopatra pointed to the carpet on which she had been pacing.

"The carpet, Your Majesty?" Her attendant appeared perplexed, but no sooner had he uttered the words than he blanched with fear, for only a fool would dare contradict the Queen's orders. Her short temper was well-known; it was said that the crocodiles of Egypt prayed for her safety as she kept them constantly fed with disobedient servants! Fortunately for him, the Queen appeared distracted and simply repeated, "we will leave at once."

"At once, Your Majesty." The attendant sank to his knees and began to roll up the carpet. What on earth, he thought to himself, could the Queen of Egypt want with this tattered old carpet?

Two days later in Alexandria, Caesar was busy with his generals when a centurion entered the room.

"Caesar, a gift has been delivered to you."

"A gift?" Even the mighty Caesar was curious when he received a gift. "A gift? What kind of gift?"

"A carpet."

"Oh, is that all?"

"The person who has brought it insists that it be delivered to you personally, claiming that it contains an invaluable treasure."

"That is what they all say," Caesar sighed wearily. "Very well. Let us

have a look at this invaluable treasure."

A few minutes later a Roman soldier came into Caesar's presence carrying a carpet which he unrolled at the Roman General's feet. To his great astonishment, out rolled Cleopatra! In an instant she was on her feet, smiling; she extended her hand in greeting.

"My apologies, mighty Caesar, for such an unorthodox entry, but there is a high price on my head."

"And what a lovely head it is," Caesar replied graciously, escorting her to a nearby seat. Such a dramatic entrance could not fail to charm him, and it was not long before Caesar had fallen deeply in love with this courageous and enchanting queen. He was a man of great intelligence and strength of personality and, although he was twice her age she, too, fell in love. Caesar restored Cleopatra to her throne and presented her with the island of Cyprus as a gift.

While in Egypt Caesar sailed down the famous Nile River with his beloved queen. Their splendid and luxurious floating palace, accompanied by a flotilla of boats, was made from beautifully carved wood from the cedars of Lebanon and decked in the finest silks.

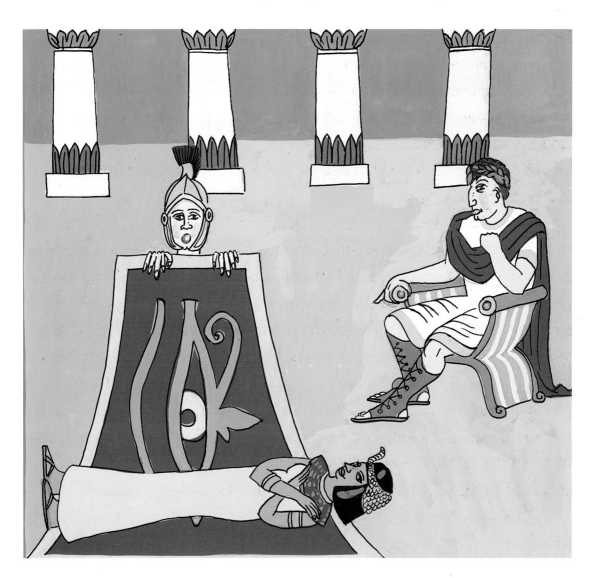

On this wonderful ship, Caesar told Cleopatra that he had visited Egypt once before when he was thirty-two years old. He had gone to Alexandria to the tomb of Alexander the Great. On seeing the famous tomb, he had burst into tears and cried out that by the age of thirty-two Alexander had conquered the whole known world and that he, Caesar, was nothing but a young senator. Cleopatra laughed and told him that he need not worry, that he was now famous throughout the world and that history would never forget the name of Julius Caesar. Little could she have imagined that it would not forget the name of Cleopatra either!

For one idyllic year Caesar stayed in Egypt and, before he returned to Rome, he was delighted to learn that Cleopatra was expecting his child. He made her promise to come and visit him in Rome after the child was born.

Not long after Caesar's departure, Cleopatra gave birth to a healthy baby boy whom she named Caesarion – Little Caesar. Later on Cleopatra and her son made their state visit to Rome where Caesar welcomed them in splendour and installed them in one of his palaces. It was a joyful time for all – Caesar was the most powerful man in the whole world and Cleopatra was secure on her throne. They were blessed with a healthy son and heir to all that Egypt and Rome could offer. All seemed well in the world – but a great tragedy was about to strike.

Caesar had made many enemies during his rise to power and he was aware that his life was in danger. However, he ignored any threats and decided to address the Senate to calm any fears that he had become too powerful and was planning to become a dictator. The day chosen for this address was the fateful 15th of March – forever known as the "Ides of March". As he climbed the steps of the Senate, he was approached by a group of men. Initially, he feared for his safety but relaxed when he spotted Brutus, whom he considered a son. But in a flash daggers were drawn and Caesar was attacked and stabbed to death, falling down the steps of the Senate.

The news of the murder of Caesar spread like wildfire through Rome until it reached the ears of Cleopatra. At first she dismissed it as mere rumour – for how could the mighty Julius Caesar be dead? But when she realized that in fact it was the truth, she knew that she had to act quickly. Her life was in danger and that of her son even more so, for those who had slain Caesar would not hesitate to kill his heir. At once Cleopatra fled Rome and headed for Egypt.

A power struggle now broke out in Rome. On one side there was Mark Antony, Caesar's old friend and comrade-in-arms, on the other a sickly nephew of Caesar by the name of Octavian who claimed that he was Caesar's rightful heir. At first, Antony and Octavian were allies, together defeating and killing Caesar's assassins at the Battle of Philippi in 42 B.C., but then they turned against each other. After many years of civil war between them, one more battle had to be fought: and to the victor the prize was nothing less than the Roman Empire.

Antony was ambitious to add more land to his territories. He looked east towards Persia, but first he knew he had to control Egypt, the gateway to the east and also the producer of the vast quantities of grain which were needed to feed his troops. Of course, he was aware of Cleopatra, and had often teased Caesar that he had met her before him when, as a dashing young cavalryman, he had fought a brilliant campaign in Egypt and helped restore her father to the throne.

Antony now wrote to Cleopatra asking her to meet him at Tarsus in southern Turkey. At first, Cleopatra made him wait, as befitting her position as Queen; but then she set off with an entourage of dazzling beauty and magnificence. The sails of the barge upon which she set off were perfumed so that, as the wind caught them, heavenly aromas were

released. The oars were of silver and the pavilion in which Cleopatra reclined was of pure gold leaf that glittered in the sunshine. The Queen herself was dressed like a goddess, and was surrounded by young boy attendants, like smiling cupids, some burning incense, others fanning her. Cleopatra took great pride in her appearance. She used oils and balsams to protect her skin against the hot, dry sun, and she was an expert in the art of perfume-making. No longer was this the young woman who had rolled herself up in a carpet to be sent to Caesar. Here was a mighty queen in all her magnificent splendour.

Antony could not fail to be impressed – for it was rare that he was upstaged. He now invited her to dine with him – only to be turned down. The Queen of Egypt did not accept invitations to dine, but was happy to extend one to him. Antony knew that he had met his match and he graciously accepted.

At first the dinner was formal and tense. Antony was uncertain of Cleopatra's loyalties, and she wished to protect her country and her son. But soon, under the bright stars of the indigo sky, Cupid's arrows could not fail to hit their targets. Cleopatra realized that, although she had given her love to Caesar, her heart belonged to Mark Antony. So began one of the greatest love stories in history.

This was an age of war, though, not of love, and neither Antony nor Cleopatra could ignore the threat of Octavian who had gathered a large fleet in preparation for an attack. Cleopatra now threw all her energies into helping Antony gather together a fleet, commanding that the cedars of Lebanon be chopped down in order to build ships. But it soon became clear that the fire of battle had gone out of Antony. Perhaps it was his love for Cleopatra, or perhaps he had simply fought too many battles – who knows? In any case he lacked the hunger and ambition of Octavian, and prepared for the decisive battle as if he knew already that his fate was doomed. Cleopatra, with all her intelligence must have sensed it also, but, loyal in her love for him, she stood by him until the shattering moment when they heard that their forces had been crushed at the Battle of Actium in 31 B.C.

At this time Antony and Cleopatra were in Alexandria and when the news reached them of their defeat, they knew that all was lost. Cleopatra pleaded with Antony to flee, for he could expect no mercy. But Antony had lost the will to live. On the very day that Octavian's troops entered Alexandria he decided he had no choice but to take his own life. He fell on his sword and died in the arms of his beloved Cleopatra. Upon this scene of grief came Octavian's centurions who at once seized Cleopatra, preventing her from committing suicide. She was brought to Octavian who expected

her to plead for her life, but was instead confronted by a proud and defiant queen. In the room with Octavian was Cleopatra's treasurer who had defected and was busy reading out a list of her wealth. Excusing herself with great dignity, Cleopatra approached the treasurer and promptly slapped him across the face, causing him to fall back in shock and Octavian to laugh out loud. He now understood why two great men such as Caesar and Antony had fallen in love with this fiery queen.

Cleopatra then turned to Octavian and asked permission to visit Antony's grave. He agreed, but gave strict orders that she should be watched at all times and prevented from taking her life. But he had not allowed for Cleopatra's cunning, for she had made secret arrangements. At Antony's grave a basket of figs, in which an asp was hidden whose bite was deadly, was delivered to her by a servant. Before Ocatvian's guards realized what was happening, Cleopatra succeeded in barring all the doors and allowed the asp to bite her. By the time the doors were knocked down, it was too late. Cleopatra was dead.

When news of Cleopatra's death reached Octavian, his anger quickly turned to sorrow, for he realized that a great queen and a formidable enemy had died. Later he would claim that Rome, in its glorious history, had only ever feared two people: the first was the great general from Carthage,

Hannibal; the other was Cleopatra of Egypt who had used her courage and intelligence as formidably as Hannibal had used his elephants.

And so, Octavian, this frail, sickly young man, had survived the ravages of the civil wars and had outlived all his rivals. The bloodshed was almost over. Almost, for there was one more cruel act to be carried out – Cleopatra's son, Caesarion, had to be put to death, for there could be no rival heirs to Caesar's name. Octavian now returned to Rome and changed his name to one more befitting that of an Emperor – Augustus.

However, before departing Egypt, he gave instructions that Cleopatra, the Queen of Kings and the last Queen of Egypt, be buried next to Antony, declaring that no grave would ever contain a pair so noble.

# CLEOPATRA

70 B.C. -   Cleopatra is born in Alexandria.

51 B.C. -   Cleopatra becomes Queen of Egypt.

50 B.C. -   Cleopatra flees to Ascalon in Palestine after a revolt against her.

48 B.C. -   Cleopatra is restored to her throne by Caesar.

47 B.C. -   Cleopatra gives birth to Caesar's son – Caesarion.

44 B.C. -   Caesar is murdered in Rome.

41 B.C. -   Cleopatra and Antony meet in Tarsus, Turkey.

31 B.C. -   Cleopatra and Antony's fleet is destroyed at Actium.

30 B.C. -   Cleopatra, aged 40, kills herself with an asp bite.

# HEROES FROM THE EAST

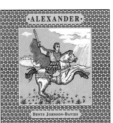

SALADIN
MARION KHALIDI

SINAN
EMMA CLARK

QUEEN OF SHEBA
MARION KHALIDI

AKBAR
JULIA MARSHALL

CHENG HO
JULIA MARSHALL

ALEXANDER
DENYS JOHNSON-DAVIES

AVICENNA
REZA SHAH-KAZEMI

RUMI
DENYS JOHNSON-DAVIES

RAZIA
WARRIOR QUEEN OF INDIA

CLEOPATRA
QUEEN OF KINGS

MEHMET
THE CONQUEROR